SEASONS OF TOGETHERNESS

A Relationship of Shared Evolution

Author

V. Chenchu Krishna Reddy

SEASONS OF TOGETHERNESS

A Relationship of Shared Evolution

This book is a work of non-fiction based on conceptual analysis, systems thinking, and philosophical interpretation of human relationships. It does not constitute psychological, medical, legal, or therapeutic advice. The author is not a licensed mental health professional. Readers are encouraged to seek qualified professional support where appropriate.

Any resemblance to actual persons, living or dead, or to real events is purely coincidental. The ideas expressed are intended for reflective and educational purposes only.

First Edition: 2026

ISBN: 978-93-5619-556-1

Author & Publisher:
V. Chenchu Krishna Reddy

Printed and published independently.

Manufactured in India.

DEDICATION

To those who are willing to question inherited forms
Without rejecting human connection.

To individuals who understand That relationships, like living systems,
Must be evaluated by alignment, Contribution, and
growth-Not by obligation or fear.

To those who seek togetherness
Not as possession, But as a shared process of evolution.

And to those who recognize
That separation, when guided by clarity,
Is not failure, But the natural completion
Of a fulfilled system.

AUTHOR'S NOTE

My academic background is in Agriculture and Geoinformatics-disciplines that observe how systems grow, align, change, and conclude over time. In these sciences, continuity is never assumed. Systems are understood through their function, their conditions, and their capacity to evolve.

Over time, this perspective extended naturally into how I observed human relationships.

Emotion and science are often treated as separate domains. With maturity, this separation becomes less convincing. Emotion also follows patterns. It emerges, stabilizes, shifts, and sometimes dissolves. When observed across time, relationships reveal structure, direction, and limits—much like any living system.

This book approaches relationships from that understanding.

It is not written for those who view emotions or relationships as obstacles to progress, nor for those who wish to disengage from human connection. It is written for individuals who recognize that relationships are part of human evolution and deserve clarity rather than confusion.

The idea presented here is simple. A relationship need not be based on love, attraction, marriage, sex, or dependency. It may exist as long as it supports shared evolution. Continuation is a conscious choice. Conclusion is a valid outcome when alignment no longer exists.

The title Seasons of Togetherness reflects this view. Togetherness, like any living process, has phases. It begins, develops, stabilizes, and may naturally conclude. Meaning is found not in permanence, but in alignment within the appropriate season.

This book offers a structured framework for examining human relationships as evolving systems—allowing togetherness to be entered with **awareness,** sustained through **alignment,** and concluded responsibly when shared evolution is no longer present.

TABLE OF CONTENTS

Introduction 1

PHASE I GENESIS

The Problem of Undesigned Bonds 2
When Effort Hides the Real Problem 4
When Silence Becomes Normal 6
When Intimacy Exists Without Understanding 8
When Intimacy Becomes Pressure 10
Marriage and Modern Dating Without Understanding 12
The Cost of Beginning Without Thought 14

PHASE II ALIGNMENT

What Alignment Actually Means 18
Emotional Alignment vs Directional Alignment 20
Early Signals of Alignment and Misalignment 23
Testing Alignment Without Pressure 25
Sexual Alignment Without Pressure 27
Sustaining Alignment as Life Changes 29
Choosing Direction Consciously 31

PHASE III CULTIVATION

Growing Together Without Control 33
Communication as Nourishment 36
Conflict Without Control 38
Shared Evolution Without Sacrifice 40
When Cultivation Ends and Drift Begins 42
Care Without Possession 44

PHASE IV DRIFT

When Paths Begin to Separate — 45
The Quiet Signals of Separation — 47
Guilt, Fear, and Staying Too Long — 49
Ending Without Blame — 51
Honouring Change — 53

PHASE V COMPLETION

Ending With Wholeness — 54
Emotional Closure Without Blame — 56
Sexual and Psychological Recovery — 58
Integrating Lessons Without Bitterness — 60
Leaving Without Carrying — 62
Connection After Understanding — 63
Relationships Beyond Dependency — 65
Shared Evolution as a Conscious Choice — 67
The Future of Human Connection — 69

THE SHARED EVOLUTION RELATIONSHIP MODEL — 72

EARTH'S REQUIREMENT FOR A NEW FORM OF HUMAN RELATIONSHIP — 73

INTRODUCTION

Human relationships shape our lives more than most things, yet we rarely stop to understand how they work.

Most relationships begin with feeling. They continue through habit. Over time, they survive on expectation. When difficulties arise, we focus on emotion and blame, while the deeper structure remains unseen. As a result, the same patterns repeat, even when the people involved change.

This book starts with a simple thought:

When the same outcomes appear again and again, the cause is not personal—it is structural.

In nature, nothing grows without conditions. In space, no path remains fixed forever. Growth depends on alignment, timing, and change. Human relationships are also living systems, yet they are often treated as permanent by assumption.

We are taught that lasting longer means succeeding, that holding on proves commitment, and that ending means failure. These ideas belong to another time. Today, lives evolve faster. Paths shift. What once fit may no longer align.

This book does not try to remove emotion from relationships.

It tries to place emotion within understanding.

Here, relationships are seen as processes, not promises. Togetherness exists while growth is shared. When growth separates, conclusion becomes natural rather than painful.

The pages that follow explore this idea step by step—how relationships begin, how they grow, how they drift, and how they can end without loss of meaning.This book is not about holding on.It is about knowing when togetherness truly belongs.

PHASE I

GENESIS

The Problem of Undesigned Bonds

Most relationships do not weaken because of one big mistake.

They weaken slowly, long before anyone realises what is happening.

Many bonds begin through feeling, comfort, or chance. Togetherness forms easily. From that moment, continuation is taken for granted. Very little thought is given to what this relationship is meant to support as life moves forward.

This quiet assumption decides everything that follows.

"What begins without clarity
moves forward without direction."

In science, no system is judged without understanding its conditions.

In agriculture, a seed grows only when soil, water, temperature, and season support it. A seed may sprout in poor conditions, but it cannot grow fully. This is not called failure. It is understood as limitation.

Human relationships are rarely seen this way.

When problems appear, attention turns to emotion, effort, or personal fault. Two people may be sincere, caring, and committed, yet still feel confusion and tiredness. This does not always mean something is wrong with them. Often, it means the bond itself was never clearly understood in relation to their changing lives.

"Good intentions cannot replace understanding."

Life does not stay the same. Responsibilities increase. Priorities change. Awareness grows. Paths that once felt shared slowly begin to separate. When a relationship has no clear way to adjust to this movement, tension appears.

Nature explains this clearly.

Rivers do not change course suddenly. They shift slowly as the land beneath them changes. The movement is quiet, gradual, and natural.

Human lives move in the same way.

When lives begin to move differently, togetherness requires adjustment. Without shared understanding, this adjustment feels like loss rather than growth.

"Distance is rarely sudden;
it grows quietly over time."

At this stage, more effort is often made. More compromise. More emotional energy. Yet the return becomes smaller.

In crop science, this is well known. When more input produces less yield, the system is no longer healthy. It continues to function, but with less life.

Relationships show the same pattern.

Togetherness remains, but it no longer adds strength or growth. The bond survives through effort, not balance.

"When effort increases
and meaning decreases,
imbalance is present."

The universe offers the same lesson. Planets remain stable only while forces stay balanced. When balance changes, movement changes. Stability is not emotional; it depends on conditions.

Human bonds also depend on balance.

When balance fades, emotion carries the pressure. Emotion turns into effort. Effort turns into exhaustion. The relationship continues, but growth stops.

At this point, many ask how the relationship can be repaired.

A more useful question comes earlier:

Was there ever clear understanding of what this togetherness was meant to support?

Genesis begins with this awareness.

Not to place blame.

But to recognise that many struggles start at the beginning, long before they are felt.

"What is not understood at the start
returns as confusion at the end."

PHASE I

GENESIS

When Effort Hides the Real Problem

When togetherness begins to feel difficult, the first response is usually effort.

People try harder.
They give more time.
They adjust more.
They compromise more.
Effort feels like the right answer, because effort is visible.

For a while, this works. Tension reduces. Calm returns. The relationship appears stable again. This creates a false sense of progress.

But effort does not always solve the problem.

Sometimes, it only hides it.

In many systems, effort can delay collapse, but it cannot correct imbalance.

In agriculture, adding more water to unsuitable soil may keep a plant alive for some time. Leaves remain green. Growth continues slowly. Yet the roots do not strengthen. The underlying condition remains unchanged.

Relationships follow the same pattern.

More effort keeps togetherness alive, but it does not restore growth. The bond survives, but it does not improve. What changes is the cost.

"When survival needs constant effort, something deeper is missing."

As effort increases, ease disappears.
Simple conversations require care.
Small differences require explanation.
Time together requires planning rather than flow.
Togetherness becomes something that must be managed.

This stage is often misunderstood as maturity. People tell themselves that all relationships require work. While this is partly true, constant effort without renewal is a warning sign.

In healthy systems, effort supports growth.

In strained systems, effort replaces it.

Geoscience explains this clearly. When natural flow is blocked, pressure builds elsewhere. The system adapts temporarily, but tension accumulates. Without release, stress eventually finds another outlet.

Human bonds behave the same way.
Unspoken thoughts increase.
Unexpressed needs grow.
Resentment develops quietly.

Because effort keeps the relationship functioning, these signs are ignored. The bond continues, but the cost is carried silently.

"When effort replaces clarity,
fatigue replaces joy."

Over time, people become tired without knowing why. Togetherness feels heavy, even though care remains. The relationship is not broken, but it is no longer light.

This is a critical stage in undesigned bonds.
The problem is no longer emotional.
It is no longer situational.
It is structural.

Genesis highlights this moment because many relationships stay here for years. They function. They survive. They appear stable.

But survival is not the same as growth.

Recognising when effort is hiding the real problem is an important step before any true change can occur.

PHASE I

GENESIS

When Silence Becomes Normal

When effort continues for a long time, another change appears quietly.

Silence begins to grow.
This silence is not the absence of words.
It is the absence of meaning.

Conversations still happen. Daily matters are discussed. Plans are made. But important thoughts are softened, delayed, or left unspoken. Not because they are unimportant, but because speaking them feels risky.

Silence becomes a form of protection.

People avoid certain topics to preserve peace. Differences are noticed, but not explored. Questions are felt, but not asked. Togetherness continues, but understanding stops expanding.

This silence is often misunderstood as comfort.
In reality, it is caution.
In natural systems, silence has a similar meaning.

In agriculture, when soil stops responding to inputs, the field appears calm. There is no visible crisis. Yet beneath the surface, nutrients are depleted. Life continues, but vitality is low.

Human relationships reflect the same condition.

Silence appears when expressing truth feels heavier than carrying it. Over time, this creates distance—not physical, but emotional and mental.

*"Silence does not mean agreement.
It often means avoidance."*

As silence becomes normal, individuals begin to live parallel lives. Togetherness exists in routine, but inner worlds separate. Growth happens privately rather than together.

This stage is especially difficult to recognise, because nothing seems wrong on the surface.

There are no major conflicts.
No dramatic endings.
No clear reason to leave.
Yet something essential is missing.

In geoscience, systems under long-term stress do not always break immediately. They adjust internally. Pressure redistributes. Stability is maintained, but energy is trapped.

Relationships behave the same way.
Unspoken thoughts accumulate.
Unmet needs deepen.
Understanding thins.
Silence holds everything together—temporarily.
But silence also prevents renewal.

Without shared expression, togetherness loses flexibility. Any change feels disruptive. Any growth feels dangerous. The bond becomes fragile, not because it is weak, but because it has stopped adapting.

"When silence replaces dialogue,
Distance grows without movement."

Genesis emphasises this stage because many relationships remain here for years. They function quietly. They appear stable. From the outside, nothing seems broken.

Inside, however, evolution has paused.

Understanding when silence has become normal is essential. It reveals how undesigned bonds maintain form while losing life.

Recognising this stage prepares the ground for the next phase, where alignment—or the absence of it—becomes impossible to ignore.

PHASE I

GENESIS

When Intimacy Exists Without Understanding

In many undesigned bonds, intimacy appears early.
Emotional closeness forms.
Physical closeness follows.
The relationship feels complete.
But intimacy is often mistaken for clarity.

"Closeness is not the same as understanding."

Sexual connection can be strong even when direction is weak. Desire creates bonding. Physical intimacy releases attachment hormones. This creates a sense of security, even when long-term alignment is unclear.

Science explains this well.

Neurobiology shows that sexual intimacy strengthens emotional attachment through chemical bonding. This attachment feels like stability, but it does not define purpose, boundaries, or shared direction.

As a result, the relationship feels deep, even when it is undefined.

"Attachment can feel like meaning when meaning has not yet formed."

In real life, this creates confusion.

Two people may share intense physical connection, regular intimacy, and emotional comfort, yet struggle when decisions arise—about future plans, values, responsibilities, or growth. The bond feels strong in private moments, but fragile when life demands clarity.

This is not contradiction.

It is imbalance.

In agriculture, early flowering does not guarantee harvest. A plant may flower beautifully under stress, using stored energy, even when soil conditions cannot support fruit. The appearance of success hides structural weakness.

Human relationships show the same pattern.
Strong intimacy creates confidence.
Life challenges expose uncertainty.

"Intensity can hide fragility."

Over time, sexual intimacy begins to serve a different role. It becomes a method of reassurance. Physical closeness is used to smooth conflict, reduce tension, or avoid difficult conversations.

Intimacy becomes maintenance.
This is not unhealthy by intention.
It is compensatory by nature.

"When clarity is missing,
intimacy is asked to hold the bond together."

As this continues, dissatisfaction appears quietly. Desire may fluctuate. Physical closeness may feel routine or pressured. One partner may seek intimacy for connection, while the other seeks it for stability.

Misunderstanding grows.

In systems science, this is known as role overload. When one component performs functions beyond its purpose, efficiency declines and strain increases.

Sexual connection was never meant to carry
direction,
decision,
and future planning.

"Intimacy connects bodies.
It cannot align lives."

At this stage, many people feel confused.
They ask,
"How can something that feels so close
feel so uncertain?"
The answer lies at the beginning.

Intimacy formed before understanding.
Attachment formed before clarity.
Togetherness formed before awareness.
This is a defining feature of undesigned bonds.

Genesis highlights this not to judge intimacy,

but to place it in context.

Without shared understanding, even the deepest connection struggles to support growth.

"What begins with closeness
must later face clarity."

PHASE I

GENESIS

When Intimacy Becomes Pressure

In some relationships, togetherness does not collapse loudly.
It tightens quietly.
Mental pressure begins not through force,
But through expectation.
One partner begins to control closeness.
Attention becomes conditional.
Affection is given or withdrawn to influence behaviour.
This pressure is rarely named.
It is felt.

*"When intimacy is used as leverage,
Freedom quietly disappears."*

Emotional blackmail often wears a gentle face.
It appears as guilt.
As sacrifice.
As unspoken demand.

*Phrases like "after everything I've done" or
"if you really cared" are not threats,
But they create pressure all the same.*

In psychology, this is recognised as coercive bonding.
Attachment is used to guide behaviour,
Not understanding.

Sexual intimacy can also become a tool.
Not through violence,
But through obligation.

**Physical closeness is expected to maintain peace.
Refusal creates tension.
Consent becomes silent compliance.**

*"When saying no feels dangerous,
Intimacy is no longer free."*

This creates deep internal conflict. The body participates. The mind resists. The self feels divided. Over time, desire weakens. Not because attraction is gone, but because safety is lost.

In neuroscience, desire is closely linked to autonomy. When autonomy is reduced, The nervous system shifts from connection to defence. Intimacy may continue, But it no longer nourishes. After separation, the impact becomes clearer. Many individuals carry intimacy-related confusion after a breakup. Trust feels fragile. Desire feels disconnected. Closeness triggers anxiety rather than comfort.

This is not weakness.
It is consequence.

"What was once used to control
Takes time to feel safe again."

Some experience numbness. Some avoid closeness. Some seek validation without connection. These are not moral failures. They are adaptive responses.

In stress biology, the body remembers pressure Even after the situation ends. Healing is not instant. Relearning safety takes time. Society rarely speaks about this cost.

Breakups are discussed emotionally, but their impact on sexuality and intimacy is often ignored. People are told to "move on" without understanding what was taken.

"Sexual healing requires safety,
not speed."

Genesis includes this truth because it reveals how undesigned bonds do not only affect emotions, but deeply shape the nervous system.

Mental pressure does not always leave marks. But it leaves patterns. Recognising these patterns is essential before any future alignment is possible.

PHASE I

GENESIS

Marriage and Modern Dating Without Understanding

Undesigned bonds appear in different forms. Marriage and modern dating reveal them clearly. In marriage, togetherness is often formalised early. Commitment is declared.

Roles are assumed.
Stability is expected.

Yet many marriages begin without shared clarity about life direction. Partners may agree on affection and loyalty, but remain unclear about growth, priorities, or long-term paths.

"Commitment can formalise togetherness,
But it cannot create understanding."

Over time, life changes. Careers shift. Responsibilities increase. Personal growth takes different shapes.

When a marriage lacks shared understanding, adjustment becomes difficult. Discussions about money, location, family roles, or personal goals turn into repeated conflict—not because partners are unwilling, but because expectations were never aligned at the start.

This creates a common pattern:
The marriage continues,
But conversations circle the same ground.

In agriculture, this resembles planting a long-duration crop without assessing water availability. The field survives early stages, but stress appears later. Maintenance increases, yield declines, and frustration grows.

Marriage behaves the same way when clarity is missing.

"Stability without direction
Becomes pressure over time."

Modern dating shows a different version of the same issue.

Dating today often begins quickly.

Connection is immediate.
Communication is constant.
Choices feel abundant.

People connect through apps, messages, and short interactions. Emotional and physical closeness may develop before shared understanding. The relationship feels active, yet undefined.

"Speed can feel like progress When direction is unclear."

In many modern bonds, togetherness continues without clear intention. Partners avoid defining the relationship to preserve freedom or avoid discomfort. As a result, expectations remain unspoken.

One person may seek progression.
The other may seek experience.
Both remain uncertain, yet attached.
This uncertainty creates silent strain.

In systems science, undefined boundaries increase instability. When limits are unclear, components interfere with one another. Efficiency drops. Tension rises.

Modern relationships reflect this exactly.
More communication does not bring clarity.
More connection does not create certainty.
More time does not guarantee direction.

"Undefined bonds create endless questions."

In both marriage and modern dating, the problem is not tradition or change.

It is the same underlying issue:

Togetherness formed without shared understanding.

One appears stable but feels heavy.
The other appears free but feels uncertain.

Both struggle for the same reason.

Genesis highlights these examples to show that undesigned bonds are not limited to one type of relationship. They exist wherever closeness begins before clarity.

*"Different forms,
Same foundation."*

Before alignment can be examined, this pattern must be recognised. Otherwise, relationships continue in form while weakening in function.

PHASE I

GENESIS

The Cost of Beginning Without Thought

After intimacy becomes pressure, After marriage becomes obligation, And after modern bonds become uncertain, Another force quietly enters the relationship. Society.

Relationships are never lived in isolation.

They are **watched.**

Judged.

Compared.

Families ask questions.

Friends give opinions.

Culture sets expectations.

Staying is praised.

Leaving is questioned.

This pressure changes behaviour.

People remain together not only for each other, But to avoid explanation, Shame, Or social discomfort.

"What society rewards,
People protect-even at personal cost."

Under this pressure, bonds harden, fear replaces honesty, appearance becomes more important than truth. At this stage, partners often begin to use What they know about each other As leverage, not always openly, often quietly.

Emotional blackmail appears as guilt.
Sacrifice is counted.
Past support is used as debt.

"I stayed for you."
"I gave up for you."
"You owe me."

These words may never be spoken loudly, But they shape behaviour.

"When love becomes leverage,
Freedom disappears."

Blame follows naturally, partners accuse each other of changing, of becoming distant, of no longer trying.

Yet both remember something uncomfortable Even in the first meeting,

Even in the early days,

There were signs.

Different priorities.

Different note of seriousness.

Different sense of life.

These signs were felt, but ignored, attraction was strong, closeness felt good.

Time was expected to solve the rest.

"What is recognised early
Is often denied until it hurts."

Psychology explains this clearly, in early bonding, the brain prioritises connection over evaluation, dopamine and attachment. Chemicals reduce critical assessment, signals are noticed, but downgraded.

Later, when reality asserts itself, those same signals return as conflict, partners blame each other for what both quietly knew.

This creates a painful loop.

One partner feels trapped.

The other feels betrayed.

Both feel misunderstood.

In systems science, this is called mutual misattribution, each component blames the other for outcomes created by the system itself, relationships behave the same way.

The bond was never clear.
The pressure was never discussed.
Yet responsibility is personalised.

"Shared confusion
Becomes personal accusation."

Society reinforces this pattern, People are taught to ask.

"Who failed?"

Instead of,

"What was never understood?"

As a result, ending feels like guilt, and staying feels like duty, Mental pressure increases, sexual life suffers, desire becomes tense or absent, closeness feels unsafe.

After separation,

The effects remain.

Trust feels fragile.

Intimacy feels complicated.

The body remembers pressure

Even when the bond has ended.

Neuroscience confirms this, The nervous system stores experiences of coercion As threat memory, safety must be relearned, healing takes time.

These outcomes are not rare.

They are common.

They occur not because people are careless,

But because beginnings are rushed

And clarity is postponed.

This is the true cost of undesigned bonds.

Not the ending.

Not the separation.

But the confusion,

The blame,

The pressure,

And the quiet loss of self.

"What begins without understanding
Demands payment later."

PHASE I has not been about judging relationships.

It has been about observing them honestly, because no bond can grow consciously until its unconscious beginnings are understood, GENESIS ends here.

Not with solutions.

Not with advice.

But with awareness.

Because awareness is the moment where repetition stops and choice becomes possible.

"Most relationship pain
Is not caused by endings,
But by beginnings
That were never clearly understood."

PHASE II

ALIGNMENT

What Alignment Actually Means

Alignment begins with a simple shift, from feeling to understanding, from assumption to observation.

In relationships, alignment is often misunderstood.

It is confused with attraction.

It is mistaken for agreement.

It is assumed to mean similarity.

Alignment is none of these.

"Alignment is not about being the same.
It is about moving without resistance."

Two people can be deeply attracted and still be misaligned, they can share affection, care, and intimacy, yet struggle when life demands direction.

Alignment exists when two lives can move forward

without forcing adjustment,

without silent sacrifice,

and without fear of change.

In science, alignment is measured by coherence, in physics, motion remains stable when forces act in compatible directions.

In agriculture, growth remains healthy when plant needs match soil and climate.

In geoscience, paths remain steady when terrain and movement agree.

Human relationships follow the same principle.

When two people are aligned,

effort supports growth.

When they are not, effort compensates for mismatch.

"Effort should nourish connection, not hold it together."

Alignment does not remove difference.

It provides space for it.

Disagreement is possible without threat, change is possible without collapse, individual growth is possible without guilt.

This is why aligned bonds feel lighter, even when life is demanding.

Alignment can be observed early.

How decisions are discussed.

How boundaries are respected.

How growth is responded to.

How conflict is handled.

These signals appear long before commitment, they are often noticed, but ignored.

Alignment asks that they be taken seriously.

"What is visible early deserves attention early."

Many people wait for certainty, alignment does not require certainty.

It requires honesty.

Honesty about values.

Honesty about direction.

Honesty about capacity.

This honesty does not end relationships, it clarifies them.

Some bonds strengthen.

Some bonds reveal limits.

Both outcomes are healthy.

Alignment is not about permanence, it is about suitability.

PHASE II continues by showing

how alignment is recognised,

how it is tested,

and how it is maintained

without control or pressure.

PHASE II

ALIGNMENT

Emotional Alignment vs Directional Alignment

Many relationships feel aligned because emotions match, care is mutual, attraction is shared, comfort is present.

This creates a sense of unity.

But emotional harmony alone

Does not guarantee alignment.

"Feeling close is not the same
As moving together."

Emotional alignment is about how people connect.

Directional alignment is about where their lives are going.

Both matter.

But they serve different purposes.

Emotional alignment creates warmth.

It supports affection, empathy, and intimacy, directional alignment supports movement, it shapes decisions, priorities, and long-term choices.

When emotional alignment exists

Without directional alignment,

Relationships feel good in the present

But struggle with the future.

In science, this distinction is clear, in physics, energy can be shared without shared direction, two forces may be strong, yet pull in different ways.

In agriculture, healthy plants may grow well early,

But if their growth pattern does not match climate or season,

Long-term yield suffers.

Human relationships follow the same rule.

Two people may love deeply and still want different lives.

Different pace.

Different values.

Different definitions of fulfilment.

This does not mean anyone is wrong.

"Misalignment is not failure.
It is information."

Problems arise when emotional alignment

Is used to ignore directional differences.

People say,

"Love will adjust."
"Time will fix it."
"We will manage somehow."

These beliefs delay clarity.

Over time, emotional alignment

Is asked to carry decisions

It was never meant to hold.

Conflict increases.

Frustration grows.

Silence returns.

Not because love faded,

But because direction was never shared.

In aligned relationships, emotional and directional alignment support each other, care remains strong, and choices feel natural, effort supports growth, not compensation.

"When direction is shared,
Emotion feels safe."

Directional alignment can be observed early.

How each person talks about the future.

How change is welcomed or resisted.

How growth in one person

Is received by the other, these signals appear quietly, often before strong attachment forms, alignment asks that they be respected,

Not overridden by feeling.

This section prepares the ground for the next question:

How is alignment tested

Without pressure,

Without control,

And without fear?

PHASE II

ALIGNMENT

Early Signals of Alignment and Misalignment

Alignment does not appear suddenly, it reveals itself early, often within the first stages of connection.

Small signals appear quietly.

They are not dramatic.

They are ordinary.

Most people notice them.

Few take them seriously.

"What feels small at the beginning
Often becomes decisive later."

Early signals of alignment appear in response, not in promises.

How questions are answered.

How disagreement is handled.

How curiosity is shown.

How boundaries are received.

In aligned bonds, curiosity is mutual.

Differences invite discussion, not defence, growth in one person does not threaten the other, in misaligned bonds, these same moments feel tense.

Questions feel intrusive.

Differences feel uncomfortable.

Growth feels destabilising.

These reactions are not intentional.

They are directional.

In behavioural science, early responses reflect underlying values and tolerance for change, they are more reliable than words.

"Behaviour reveals direction
Before intention admits it."

Another early signal appears around decision-making.

Aligned partners discuss choices openly.

They consider impact on both lives.

They are willing to pause, adjust, or rethink.

Misaligned partners delay decisions.

They avoid clarity.

They rely on emotion or hope

To move forward without agreement.

This avoidance is often misread as flexibility.

In reality, it is uncertainty, in systems science, early instability is rarely dramatic, it shows as hesitation, inconsistency, and unclear boundaries.

Relationships behave the same way.

Alignment is also visible in how conflict feels.

In aligned bonds, disagreement feels safe.

Resolution is possible without fear.

The relationship remains steady even when opinions differ, in misaligned bonds, conflict feels threatening, issues repeat.

Silence replaces resolution.

"Alignment allows conflict
Without collapse."

One of the clearest early signals is how individuality is treated, when alignment exists, personal interests are respected, time apart does not create insecurity, independence strengthens connection.

When alignment is weak, independence creates tension, time apart raises doubt, individual growth feels risky.

These signs are not moral judgments.

They are directional indicators.

Alignment does not require perfection, it requires compatibility in movement, recognising early signals prevents later confusion, ignoring them creates it.

This section prepares the reader

For a deeper understanding of alignment:

How it is tested,

And how it is maintained

Without control or pressure.

PHASE II

ALIGNMENT

Testing Alignment Without Pressure

Alignment is not proven through promises, it is revealed through response, many people try to test relationships

By increasing intensity—

More time,

More closeness,

More commitment.

This approach often hides misalignment

Instead of revealing it.

"Pressure creates compliance,
Not clarity."

True alignment is tested in space, not in force, when space is allowed, real patterns appear, people show how they manage distance, uncertainty, and independence.

In aligned bonds, space does not create panic, connection remains steady, trust is not threatened, in misaligned bonds, space creates anxiety.

Communication becomes urgent.

Reassurance is demanded.

These reactions are not emotional weakness.

They are directional signals.

In psychology, secure systems tolerate variation, insecure systems attempt to control it, relationships behave the same way.

Another quiet test of alignment

Appears during change.

New responsibilities.

Career shifts.

Personal growth.

Unexpected challenges, aligned partners respond with curiosity.

They ask how change can be integrated.

They adapt without losing balance.

Misaligned partners resist change.

They experience growth as disruption.

They attempt to restore the old pattern.

"What cannot adapt
Will attempt to control."

Testing alignment does not require confrontation, it requires observation.

How plans are adjusted.

How needs are expressed.

How disagreement is handled

When no immediate solution exists.

In systems science, resilience is measured by how a system responds to stress, not by how it performs under ideal conditions.

Relationships are no different.

Another test appears in boundaries.

Aligned bonds respect limits

Without interpreting them as rejection.

Boundaries are seen as information,

Not as distance.

In misaligned bonds, boundaries are challenged, they are negotiated repeatedly, or quietly ignored. This creates tension, even when affection remains.

"Where boundaries are unsafe,
Alignment is weak."

Testing alignment early

Prevents later pressure.

It replaces guessing with knowing.

When alignment is present, clarity increases, when it is absent, clarity feels uncomfortable.

This discomfort is not a warning sign.

It is useful information.

PHASE II continues

By exploring how alignment,

Once recognised,

Can be sustained without effort

And without self-reduction.

PHASE II

ALIGNMENT

Sexual Alignment Without Pressure

Sexual alignment is often misunderstood, it is reduced to attraction, frequency, or performance.

In reality, sexual alignment is about safety,

mutual freedom,

and shared meaning.

"Desire grows where safety exists."

In aligned relationships, intimacy is chosen. It is not used to convince, to calm, or to hold the relationship together. Closeness feels natural, not required.

When sexual alignment exists, both partners feel free to say yes and equally free to say no, neither response creates fear.

In misaligned bonds, intimacy slowly becomes a tool. It is used to reduce tension, to avoid difficult conversations, or to restore closeness after conflict.

This creates pressure,

even when care remains.

"When intimacy carries responsibility,
desire weakens."

Neuroscience explains this clearly. Desire is supported by the nervous system when it feels safe and autonomous.

When pressure is present, the body shifts into defence, connection becomes effort.

This is why sexual difficulties often appear in relationships that look stable from the outside.

The issue is rarely physical.

It is relational.

Aligned sexual bonds allow difference.

Different rhythms.

Different needs.

Different expressions.

These differences are discussed,

not judged.

They inform understanding, not expectation. In misaligned bonds, difference becomes conflict. One partner feels rejected. The other feels obligated. Neither feels free.

"Freedom is the foundation of intimacy."

Sexual alignment is also revealed

in how intimacy changes over time.

Aligned bonds allow fluctuation.

Desire rises and falls without panic or blame. Misaligned bonds interpret change as threat.

Reassurance is demanded.

Pressure increases.

This is not desire. It is fear. Sexual alignment does not mean constant harmony. It means shared understanding.

It supports closeness

without sacrificing autonomy.

PHASE II includes this discussion

to restore intimacy to its proper place— as expression, not obligation; as connection, not currency.

This prepares the way for the final question of alignment how can alignment be sustained as

Life continues to change?

PHASE II

ALIGNMENT

Sustaining Alignment as Life Changes

Alignment is not a moment. It is a condition that must remain responsive to life. People change.

Circumstances shift.

Responsibilities increase.

Growth takes new forms. Alignment is tested not when life is calm, but when life moves.

*"Alignment survives change
When change is allowed."*

In aligned bonds, change is not feared. It is discussed. It is examined together. It is integrated without panic.

Growth in one person

Does not threaten the other.

It invites adjustment, not resistance.

In misaligned bonds, change creates tension. Growth is questioned.

New directions feel destabilising.

This difference is not emotional.

It is structural.

In systems science, sustainable systems are adaptive. they adjust parameters without losing coherence.

Rigid systems survive briefly,

Then fracture.

Human relationships follow the same law, sustaining alignment requires

Ongoing observation.

How decisions evolve.

How power is shared.

How independence is respected.

How responsibility is distributed.

Alignment weakens when these elements

Stop being discussed.

"Silence erodes alignment
Faster than conflict."

Another key factor is consent—repeated, not assumed.

Consent to change.

Consent to pace.

Consent to shared direction.

Aligned partners renew this consent naturally. They do not assume permanence. They choose continuation.

Misaligned partners rely on history.

They stay because they have stayed.

This difference defines sustainability.

Sustaining alignment does not mean

Preventing divergence.

It means recognising it early. When paths begin to separate, aligned bonds respond with honesty, not blame.

This honesty protects dignity—

Whether the bond continues

Or prepares for completion.

PHASE II closes by affirming a simple truth:

Alignment is not control.

It is cooperation with reality.

PHASE II

ALIGNMENT

Choosing Direction Consciously

PHASE II has not been about perfection. It has been about clarity. Alignment does not promise ease.

It offers coherence, when alignment exists, effort supports life, when it does not, effort replaces it.

This phase has shown that Alignment can be observed, Tested, And sustained— Without pressure, Without self-reduction, And without fear.

"Clarity is kinder than hope."

Aligned bonds feel lighter

Not because they lack challenge,

But because they lack confusion.

They allow difference without threat. Change without collapse. Intimacy without obligation.

Most importantly, they allow two lives to move forward without one being diminished.

PHASE II ends here.

Not with guarantees,

But with discernment.

Because once direction is seen clearly, the next question is inevitable, how do aligned bonds grow together over time?

That question belongs to the next phase.

PHASE III begins

Where alignment becomes practice.

Not with guarantees,

But with discernment.

Because once direction is seen clearly,

The next question is inevitable:

How do aligned bonds grow together

Over time?

That question belongs to the next phase.

PHASE III begins

Where alignment becomes practice.

PHASE III

CULTIVATION

Growing Together Without Control

Alignment makes togetherness possible. Cultivation makes it meaningful. Once direction is shared,

The question changes.

Not,

"Do we fit?"

But,

"How do we grow without losing ourselves?"

Cultivation is not about improvement.

It is about nourishment.

"What is aligned still needs care."

In relationships, cultivation means creating conditions where both lives can continue to grow

Without pressure,

Without comparison,

And without control.

Growth is not forced.

It is supported.

In agriculture, crops do not grow because they are pulled upward.

They grow because the soil is prepared,

Water is available,

And space is respected.

Human relationships follow the same principle, when conditions are healthy,

Growth happens naturally.

When control replaces care,

Growth becomes resistance.

"Growth resists force
But responds to support."

Cultivation begins with allowing difference, aligned partners do not grow in identical ways.

They grow in compatible directions.

One may change faster.

One may explore deeper.

One may pause.

Cultivation respects rhythm.

In mismanaged bonds, Difference creates insecurity. In cultivated bonds, Difference provides balance.

This balance requires trust.

Trust not as blind belief,

But as confidence in shared direction.

Cultivation also means protecting space.

Time apart.

Individual interests.

Private thoughts.

These are not threats to togetherness, they are nutrients.

"Space does not weaken connection.
It strengthens it."

In systems science, Overcrowding reduces efficiency. In ecology, Diversity increases resilience. Relationships thrive under the same conditions. Cultivation is also visible in communication.

Not constant explanation.

Not emotional processing without end.

But clear sharing,

Honest listening,

And timely adjustment.

When communication becomes maintenance, Cultivation has stopped. Cultivation keeps togetherness alive Without exhausting it.

PHASE III begins here

Because alignment without cultivation

Slowly fades.

Growth is not automatic.

It is sustained by how people choose

To live together each day.

PHASE III

CULTIVATION

Communication as Nourishment

In cultivated relationships, communication is not constant.

It is meaningful.

Communication is often misunderstood as talking more.

In reality, growth depends on talking well.

"What nourishes a bond
Is not volume,
But clarity."

Healthy communication does not aim to fix everything.

It aims to keep understanding alive.

In agriculture, overwatering damages roots.

Too much input weakens structure.

Growth requires balance.

Relationships respond the same way.

When communication becomes excessive,

Reactive,

Or repetitive,

It stops nourishing connection.

It becomes maintenance.

Cultivated communication has rhythm. Some moments require listening. Some require expression. Some require silence.

Silence, when chosen,

Is not avoidance.

It is space.

"Not every truth needs urgency.
Some need timing."

In cultivated bonds, Disagreement is welcomed early. Small differences are addressed Before they harden. This prevents accumulation. In mismanaged bonds, Issues are postponed for peace. Silence stores tension.

Later, small matters explode.

Communication also includes how emotions are shared.

In cultivated relationships, emotion is expressed without accusation.

Feelings are described,

Not assigned.

"I feel distant"

Instead of

"You make me distant."

This difference preserves dignity.

"Language can invite understanding
Or provoke defence."

Another sign of cultivated communication

Is the ability to pause.

When conversations grow intense, both partners can step back without fear of abandonment.

This pause protects clarity.

In systems science, Feedback loops keep systems stable. Without feedback, Systems drift. Communication is the feedback loop of relationships.

When it remains open,

Growth continues.

When it becomes blocked,

Cultivation stops.

This section prepares the ground for the next challenge of cultivation, how conflict can exist without turning into control.

PHASE III

CULTIVATION

Conflict Without Control

Conflict is not the enemy of growth. Control is.

In cultivated relationships, conflict is expected.

Different minds will disagree.

Different rhythms will clash.

Difference itself is not a problem.

"Growth does not require agreement.
It requires respect."

Problems arise when conflict is handled as a threat rather than information. In controlling bonds, conflict triggers defence. Voices rise. Positions harden.

Winning becomes more important than understanding.

In cultivated bonds,

Conflict slows the relationship down.

Attention increases.

Listening deepens.

The goal is not victory.

It is clarity.

In agriculture, storms are not avoided. They are planned for, fields are designed to drain water, not fight rain.

Human relationships need the same wisdom.

Conflict should pass through the bond,

Not flood it.

"What is resisted violently
Returns destructively."

Cultivated conflict has boundaries.

No threats.

No humiliation.

No emotional punishment.

Disagreement stays focused on the issue, not the identity of the person.

"I disagree with this choice"

Is different from

"You are the problem."

This distinction preserves dignity.

In psychology, this is known as Separating behaviour from self. It allows correction without damage. Control enters when one partner Tries to end conflict By overpowering the other.

Through silence.

Through anger.

Through withdrawal.

Through emotional pressure.

These methods stop the argument, But harm cultivation.

"Peace achieved through control
Costs growth."

In cultivated bonds, Conflict ends when understanding increases, Not when someone gives up.

Resolution may not be immediate.

But direction becomes clearer.

Another sign of healthy conflict Is repair.

After disagreement,

Connection is restored deliberately.

Not through intimacy as compensation,

But through conversation.

This repair builds resilience.

In systems science, Systems that recover quickly from disturbance are stronger than those that avoid disturbance. relationships are no different.

Cultivation does not remove conflict.

It transforms it From threat Into feedback.

This prepares the relationship for its most important task growing together without becoming the same.

PHASE III
CULTIVATION

Shared Evolution Without Sacrifice

Cultivation reaches its true test when both people begin to change.

Change is inevitable.

Growth is personal.

Evolution does not happen at the same speed or in the same direction.

In cultivated relationships,

This difference is not treated as danger.

"Growth should expand life,
Not demand payment from it."

Shared evolution does not mean equal change.

It means compatible change.

One partner may advance in career. Another may shift priorities. One may explore deeply. Another may stabilise. Cultivation allows these movements Without demanding symmetry.

Sacrifice is often misunderstood here.

Temporary compromise can support growth.

Permanent self-denial slowly damages it.

"Support should not require
The loss of self."

In agriculture, pruning helps a plant grow. Uprooting it to protect another plant Destroys both.

Human relationships require the same distinction, cultivated bonds support evolution by adjusting structure, not by limiting growth.

This requires honest negotiation.

What can be shared.

What must remain individual.

What needs support.

What needs space.

These conversations are not signs of weakness they are signs of maturity.

In mismanaged bonds, Growth triggers fear. One partner slows down.

The other feels guilty.

In cultivated bonds, Growth is welcomed, Even when it requires rebalancing.

"When growth is safe,
Jealousy fades."

Shared evolution also means

Allowing change in the relationship itself.

Roles may shift.

Needs may change.

Forms of closeness may evolve.

Cultivation accepts this fluidity.

In systems science, Adaptive systems survive Because they update their structure. Rigid systems collapse under pressure. Relationships are no different.

Shared evolution does not promise permanence.

It promises honesty.

It allows two lives

To grow side by side

Without one being reduced To sustain the other. This prepares the way For the next truth of cultivation.

What happens when growth directions begin to diverge.

PHASE III

CULTIVATION

When Cultivation Ends and Drift Begins

Cultivation does not fail suddenly. It fades gradually.

Not because care disappears, but because attention shifts.

Life becomes busy.

Priorities multiply.

Growth takes new forms.

Without noticing,

Maintenance replaces nourishment.

"What is not cultivated
Does not die immediately.
It drifts."

Drift begins when conversations shorten.

When curiosity fades.

When difference is tolerated

But no longer explored. There is no conflict. No crisis. Only distance.

In cultivated bonds, change is addressed early, in drifting bonds, change is postponed, silence grows again, not from fear, but from habit.

In systems science, Drift occurs when feedback loops weaken. The system continues, But coherence declines. Relationships follow the same pattern. Drift is often misunderstood as maturity.

In reality, it is unattended change.

"Distance does not always mean loss.
Sometimes it means neglect."

This stage is important because it is reversible—briefly.

Awareness can restore cultivation.

Attention can reopen communication.

Curiosity can return.

But if drift continues unexamined,

Direction eventually separates.

At that point, cultivation has completed its role.

This is not failure.

It is transition.

PHASE III closes here

Because cultivation cannot force permanence.

It can only support growth

While growth remains shared.

When growth begins to diverge,

A new phase is required.

PHASE III

CULTIVATION

Care Without Possession

PHASE III has been about care.

Not control.

Not endurance.

Cultivation succeeds when care is given freely and received without obligation, it allows growth without fear, difference without dominance, change without collapse.

"Care nourishes best
When it does not claim ownership."

Cultivation does not guarantee permanence.

It guarantees dignity.

It ensures that if togetherness continues,

It does so consciously.

And if it changes, It changes honestly.

PHASE III ends here,

Not because growth stops,

But because growth sometimes moves apart.

The next phase explores that truth.

PHASE IV begins

Where shared direction

Starts to shift.

PHASE IV

DRIFT

When Paths Begin to Separate

Drift does not announce itself, it arrives without warning, without conflict, without blame.

Two lives that once moved together

Begin to move at different speeds.

Not because care has ended,

But because direction has changed.

"Not all separation begins with pain.
Some begins with difference."

In this phase, nothing appears broken. Communication still exists. Respect remains. Routines continue.

Yet something essential has shifted.

The shared horizon no longer feels shared.

In science, drift is a natural phenomenon. Continental plates move slowly, Almost invisibly.

Over time, landscapes change

Without a single violent moment.

Human relationships follow the same law.

Drift occurs when growth continues

But alignment weakens.

Each person evolves honestly,

Yet no longer together.

This is why drift is often misunderstood.

There is no villain.

No failure.

No clear mistake.

"Drift is not betrayal.
It is divergence."

In this phase, people often feel confused. They sense distance, But cannot explain it.

Questions arise quietly:

"Why does this feel different?"

"Why do we understand each other less?"

"Why does togetherness feel heavier?"

These questions are not accusations.

They are signals.

In psychology, drift appears When internal values shift faster Than external structures.

The relationship remains unchanged

While the people do not.

This creates tension—

Not emotional,

But directional.

Drift is painful because it challenges a deep belief:

That growth together should always be possible.

But growth does not promise permanence.

It promises honesty.

PHASE IV begins here

To normalise what is rarely spoken:

That some relationships do not end

Because something went wrong,

But because something changed.

PHASE IV

DRIFT

The Quiet Signals of Separation

Drift reveals itself through small changes. Not through arguments, But through absence. Conversations become shorter. Curiosity softens. Shared excitement fades into routine.

Nothing feels wrong.

Yet nothing feels close.

"Distance does not always arrive loudly.
Sometimes it arrives politely."

In this stage, people often try harder.

They increase effort.

They recreate routines.

They seek the old feeling.

But effort cannot restore direction.

In psychology, this is known as Emotional lag. Behaviour continues, While inner alignment has already shifted.

This creates confusion.

People feel guilty for noticing distance.

They question themselves.

They wonder if they are ungrateful,

Selfish, Or impatient. Society reinforces this doubt.

"Every relationship goes through phases."

"Just adjust."

"Don't overthink."

These responses dismiss the signal instead of listening to it.

"When signals are ignored,
Clarity is delayed."

Another quiet sign of drift Is emotional politeness. Disagreements are softened.

Truths are edited.

Honesty feels unnecessary—or risky.

This politeness preserves peace,

But reduces intimacy.

In aligned bonds,

Truth strengthens connection.

In drifting bonds,

Truth threatens stability.

This is not dishonesty.

It is protection. People protect what still exists, Even as it changes.

Drift also appears in imagination.

Future plans feel abstract.

Shared dreams lose detail. Conversations about **"us"** Shift toward **"I"**.

This shift is subtle,

But significant.

In systems science, Directional change begins Before structural change.

The system feels different

Before it looks different.

Relationships follow the same path.

Recognising these signals

Does not force an ending.

It offers choice, ignoring them postpones it.

PHASE IV continues

By examining the emotional weight

That drift places on both people— Especially guilt, fear, And the pressure to pretend.

PHASE IV

DRIFT

Guilt, Fear, and Staying Too Long

As drift becomes harder to ignore, Another weight appears.

Guilt.

People feel guilty for changing.

Guilty for noticing distance.

Guilty for wanting something different

Without knowing exactly what that is.

"Guilt often appears

Before honesty is allowed."

This guilt is rarely personal, it is learned.

Society teaches people

To equate continuity with loyalty.

To question change as selfishness.

To see endurance as virtue.

As a result, many people stay longer

Than they should—

Not because they are confused,

But because they are afraid.

Fear of hurting the other.

Fear of being judged.

Fear of being wrong.

This fear slows honesty.

In psychology, this is known as Avoidance through responsibility. People carry emotional weight To avoid confronting reality.

They tell themselves,

"Nothing is wrong enough."

"We can manage."

"This phase will pass."

Sometimes it does.

Often it does not.

"Staying without clarity
Does not preserve connection.
It delays understanding."

Another layer of guilt appears When one person recognises drift Before the other.

The awareness feels unfair, silence feels safer than truth, so people wait.

They wait for certainty.

They wait for permission.

They wait for a reason strong enough

To justify change.

In the meantime,

Distance grows.

In systems science, Delay under known instability Increases long-term disruption.

The longer adjustment is postponed,

The greater the eventual cost.

Relationships follow the same pattern. Staying too long does not protect people From pain.

It often deepens it, not because separation is cruel, but because dishonesty is exhausting.

"Truth delayed
Does not disappear.
It returns heavier."

PHASE IV does not judge staying.

It observes its cost.

Understanding this cost

Is necessary before the final step:

Ending without blame,

Without damage,

And without regret.

PHASE IV

DRIFT

Ending Without Blame

When drift becomes clear,

The question is no longer

Whether something is wrong.

The question becomes How to respond without harm.

Ending is often imagined as rupture.

As rejection.

As failure.

But drift changes the nature of ending.

Here, separation is not caused by conflict,

But by divergence.

Not by lack of care,

But by change.

"Not every ending needs an enemy."

Ending without blame requires one thing above all:

Clarity without accusation.

It means recognising that two lives Can grow honestly and still grow apart.

Blame attempts to simplify this truth.

It assigns fault

To reduce discomfort.

But blame damages what drift does not:

Dignity.

In psychology, blame is a defence. It protects identity By externalising loss. Yet it prolongs pain.

In systems science, clean separation preserves structure, violent separation destroys it.

Relationships follow the same rule.

Ending without blame involves speaking plainly.

Not,

"You failed me."

But,

"We changed."

Not,

"You are the problem."

But,

"Our directions no longer match."

These statements do not erase pain.

They prevent harm.

"Truth spoken calmly
Protects both sides."

Ending without blame also respects timing.

It avoids sudden withdrawal.

It avoids emotional punishment.

It allows space for processing,

For grief,

For adjustment.

This does not mean prolonging suffering, it means ending consciously.

In drifting bonds, This kind of ending is an act of care. Care not to preserve togetherness, But to preserve humanity.

PHASE IV closes here

Because drift does not demand destruction.

It asks for recognition.

When recognition is honest,

Ending becomes transition,

Not trauma.

PHASE IV

DRIFT

Honouring Change

PHASE IV has been about change.

Not dramatic change.

Quiet change.

The kind that arrives slowly and asks to be noticed.

Drift does not mean love was false, it means growth was real.

Honouring change means accepting that not all bonds are meant to last forever, but all bonds deserve dignity.

"What ends honestly
Does not damage the past."

PHASE IV ends here.

Not with loss,

But with understanding.

Because when drift is acknowledged, The next step becomes possible: Completion without damage.

That belongs to the next phase.

PHASE V

COMPLETION

Ending With Wholeness

Completion is different from separation.

Separation focuses on distance.

Completion focuses on closure.

Most endings hurt not because they happen, But because they remain unfinished.

Words are left unsaid.

Meanings stay unclear.

Stories feel incomplete.

"What is not completed
Continues to live inside us."

Completion is the act of finishing consciously.

It allows an experience to end

Without carrying unresolved weight forward.

In psychology, incomplete emotional experiences Remain active in memory.

They resurface as patterns,

Fear,

Or repetition.

Completion releases this energy.

It does not erase pain.

It gives pain a place to settle.

Completion begins with acknowledgement.

Acknowledging what was shared.

Acknowledging what changed.

Acknowledging what could not continue.

This honesty does not weaken the past.

It gives it structure.

In natural systems, Cycles that complete properly Restore balance. Cycles that are interrupted Create instability.

Human relationships follow the same law, completion also requires restraint.

Not every truth needs to be spoken.

Not every emotion needs expression.

Not every explanation needs agreement.

"Completion is not about saying everything.
It is about saying enough."

This restraint protects dignity— Both one's own And the other's. Completion avoids rewriting history. It does not turn love into mistake, Or care into illusion.

It recognises that something real existed, even if it could not continue.

In this phase,

People often ask,

"How do I move on?"

Completion answers differently, not by moving away, but by settling what remains inside.

PHASE V begins here

To show that endings,

When handled consciously,

Do not break people.

They restore them.

PHASE V

COMPLETION

Emotional Closure Without Blame

Emotional closure is often misunderstood.

It is not agreement.

It is not forgiveness.

It is not reconciliation.

Closure is understanding without resistance.

"Closure does not require the other person.
It requires clarity within."

Many people wait for apologies, Explanations, Or validation.

When these do not come,

Closure feels impossible.

In reality, closure is an internal process. It begins by releasing the need To assign fault. Blame keeps the story active.

It ties identity to injury.

It delays peace.

In psychology, blame maintains emotional arousal. The mind remains alert, searching for justification. Energy stays trapped. Closure releases this loop.

It does not deny hurt.

It contextualises it.

"I was hurt" becomes

"I understand why this could not continue."

This shift changes everything.

"Understanding ends cycles
That anger cannot."

Emotional closure also requires Letting go of imagined futures.

Not the person, but the life that was expected.

Grieving these expectations

Is part of completion.

Without this grief,

The mind keeps returning

To what could have been.

Closure does not erase memory.

It reorganises it.

Memories move from longing to learning.

In neuroscience, This process reduces emotional charge. The nervous system exits threat mode. Safety returns gradually.

Closure is quiet.

It does not announce itself.

It shows up as ease.

Sleep improves.

Thoughts slow.

The past stops interrupting the present.

"Peace is often mistaken for forgetting.
It is actually integration."

This section prepares the ground For the next aspect of completion, how the body and sexuality recover after emotional bonds end.

PHASE V

COMPLETION

Sexual and Psychological Recovery

After emotional closure begins,

The body follows more slowly.

This delay is normal.

Intimacy does not end

When a relationship ends.

The nervous system remembers patterns Long after circumstances change.

"The body heals at its own pace,
Not at the speed of decisions."

Sexual recovery is often misunderstood As returning desire quickly. In reality, recovery means restoring safety.

Some people feel numb.

Some feel hyper-aware.

Some avoid closeness.

Some seek it without connection.

These responses are not signs of damage.

They are adaptive states.

In neuroscience, The nervous system shifts between Connection and protection.

After prolonged attachment or pressure,

Protection dominates.

Recovery happens

When safety becomes consistent again.

Safety is not created by intimacy, intimacy grows from safety.

"Desire returns

Where pressure is absent."

Psychological recovery follows a similar path. Thoughts gradually slow. Self-trust returns. Decisions feel lighter. People begin to notice themselves again— Preferences, Boundaries, Rhythms.

This reconnection is subtle,

But powerful.

In psychology, This stage is known as reintegration.

The self no longer defines itself

Through the ended bond.

Sexual identity also stabilises here.

Attraction becomes choice,

Not reaction.

Closeness feels optional,

Not urgent.

This is not indifference, it is autonomy.

Recovery does not require comparison.

It does not require replacing.

It does not require proving strength.

It requires patience.

"Healing is not progress.
It is permission."

PHASE V includes this section

To normalise recovery as a process, not a performance.

When psychological and sexual recovery Are allowed to complete naturally,

The ground becomes ready

For renewal - Without repetition.

PHASE V

COMPLETION

Integrating Lessons Without Bitterness

Completion is incomplete

If learning turns into resentment.

Many people understand what ended,

But remain angry about it.

They carry insight,

But also bitterness.

This bitterness hardens learning. It protects the self, but narrows the future.

"What is learned with bitterness
Is repeated with fear."

Integration means allowing experience

To inform wisdom

Without defining identity.

The relationship is no longer the centre.

It becomes context.

This shift is subtle.

Instead of asking,

"Why did this happen to me?"

The question becomes,

"What did this show me about myself?"

In psychology,

This is meaning-making. It allows experiences to settle without ongoing emotional charge.

Lessons integrate cleanly

When they are owned,

Not weaponised.

Not,

"I was wronged."

But,

"I see more clearly now."

This clarity does not deny pain. It places pain in proportion.

"Wisdom does not erase scars.
It prevents reopening them."

Integration also requires releasing comparison. Comparing past and future,

Self and others, what was and what could be.

Comparison keeps attention backward.

Integration moves it forward.

As lessons settle, something important happens, expectation softens. People stop searching for certainty.

They become more attentive to fit,

To direction,

To inner response.

This is not caution.

It is discernment.

Completion reaches its final stage here.

The past no longer asks for defence.

The future no longer demands urgency.

Space appears.

PHASE V closes

When experience becomes understanding and understanding becomes quiet confidence.

PHASE V

COMPLETION

Leaving Without Carrying

PHASE V has been about finishing.

Not forgetting.

Not escaping.

But completing.

Completion allows a person, to leave a chapter, without dragging it into the next.

"What is completed

Does not follow you."

This phase has shown that endings, When handled consciously, Restore energy.

They return attention to the present.

They reopen capacity.

They make renewal possible.

PHASE V ends here

Because nothing more is needed from what has already passed.

What remains is readiness.

The next phase does not look backward, it looks forward.

PHASE VI begins

Where experience becomes insight and insight prepares the ground for new beginnings.

PHASE V

COMPLETION

Connection After Understanding

Regenesis does not mean starting again, it means starting differently.

After awareness,

after alignment,

after cultivation,

after drift,

and after completion,

a person does not return to innocence. They return with insight.

"What returns is not the past,
but the capacity to choose better."

Regenesis is the phase where experience becomes intelligence.

It is not driven by urgency.

It is not driven by fear of loneliness.

It is not driven by unfinished emotion.

Connection begins here from a different place.

In science, regeneration occurs only after integration.

A system repairs itself by learning from stress, not by repeating it.

Human relationships follow the same law.

Regenesis does not seek intensity.

It seeks coherence.

It values direction over attraction.

Capacity over promise.

Stability over stimulation.

This does not reduce feeling, it refines it.

"Depth is not lost
when chaos is removed."

In this phase, people recognise patterns early.

They notice bodily responses.

They respect hesitation.

They trust clarity more than chemistry.

Regenesis allows choice without pressure. People no longer ask,

"Will this work?"

They ask,

"Does this fit?"

This question changes everything.

Connection becomes exploratory, not consumptive.

Curiosity replaces urgency.

Presence replaces projection.

Regenesis is not about finding the right person, it is about becoming a clear participant.

Clear in boundaries.

Clear in direction.

Clear in capacity.

This clarity does not harden people, it steadies them.

PHASE VI begins here

because the future of human connection depends not on better emotions, but on better understanding.

PHASE V

COMPLETION

Relationships Beyond Dependency

For much of human history, relationships have been built on need.

Need for security.

Need for belonging.

Need for survival.

Need for validation.

Dependency once made sense.

It reduced risk.

It increased continuity.

But dependency also limits evolution.

"What is needed for survival
Is not always suitable for growth."

Regenesis proposes a different foundation.

Relationships not formed to complete each other,

But to accompany each other.

Not to fill absence,

But to share direction.

In psychology, dependency forms when connection replaces self-regulation.

The bond becomes a substitute for internal stability.

This creates pressure.

Fear of loss.

Resistance to change.

Regenesis shifts the structure.

Connection no longer carries the burden of holding identity together.

Each person arrives whole, not finished, but stable.

"Wholeness reduces fear;
Clarity reduces attachment."

In this model, Relationships are chosen, Not clung to.

Closeness exists without possession.

Support exists without control.

Care exists without obligation.

This does not weaken bonds.

It strengthens them.

In systems science, Interdependent systems outperform dependent ones.

Components function independently, yet coordinate by design.

Human relationships thrive the same way.

Beyond dependency,

Conflict becomes information not threat.

Space becomes nourishment, not distance.

Change becomes dialogue, not disruption.

This also transforms intimacy.

Sexual connection is no longer used to secure attachment, it becomes expression, not reassurance.

Desire remains alive

Because freedom remains intact.

"Freedom is not the enemy of intimacy.
It is its condition."

Relationships beyond dependency do not promise permanence. They promise honesty.

People stay because it fits, not because they are afraid to leave.

This prepares the final question of Regenesis:

What kind of society emerges when relationships are built this way?

PHASE V

COMPLETION

Shared Evolution as a Conscious Choice

In Regenesis, togetherness is not assumed.

It is chosen—again and again.

Shared evolution is no longer accidental.

It is intentional.

People do not grow together because they promised permanence.

They grow together because their directions continue to align.

"Continuation is not owed.
It is renewed."

This changes the nature of commitment.

Commitment is no longer about endurance.

It is about participation.

Each person remains responsible for their own growth.

The relationship becomes a space where growth is witnessed, not managed, in evolutionary biology, cooperative systems survive when adaptation is mutual, not forced.

Species evolve together only when their changes remain compatible.

Human relationships follow the same law.

Shared evolution requires periodic honesty.

Not dramatic evaluations.

Simple questions.

Are we still moving in a direction that supports both lives?

Are we responding to change with curiosity or resistance?

Are we choosing each other, or relying on habit?

These questions do not weaken bonds.

They keep them real.

"What is examined regularly
Does not decay silently."

In this model, divergence is not treated as betrayal.

It is treated as information, when paths begin to separate.

People respond early.

They adjust,

Or they prepare to complete

With dignity.

This prevents shock.

It preserves trust.

Shared evolution also reshapes identity.

People are no longer defined by relationship status, they are defined by direction, values, and capacity for connection.

The relationship becomes a companion to life, not the container of it.

"Togetherness should walk beside life,
Not replace it."

Regenesis does not create fewer relationships.

It creates healthier ones.

It allows connection without fear,

Change without guilt,

And endings without damage.

This leads to the final reflection:

What happens to society when enough individuals

Relate this way?

PHASE V

COMPLETION

The Future of Human Connection

When enough individuals relate with awareness, relationships stop being personal struggles and begin shaping society.

The future of human connection Will not be defined by stronger emotions, But by clearer structures.

In this future, relationships are not used to escape loneliness, prove worth, or secure identity.

They are used to share life.

"The next evolution of connection
Is not emotional intensity,
But relational intelligence."

People enter relationships with self-knowledge.

They speak direction early.

They respect difference without fear.

They leave without destruction.

This changes families.

It changes communities.

It changes culture.

Marriage becomes choice, not pressure.

Partnership becomes cooperation, not obligation.

Intimacy becomes expression, not leverage.

In social science, systems stabilise when individual units function well.

Healthy individuals form resilient networks.

Human connection evolves the same way.

Conflict decreases, Not because people avoid disagreement, But because clarity reduces misunderstanding.

Separation becomes less traumatic, not because people care less, but because they complete more honestly.

This future does not reject tradition.

It refines it.

It does not reject commitment.

It makes it conscious.

*"What is chosen freely
Lasts more honestly."*

Regenesis offers no guarantees. It offers a framework.

A way to relate that respects growth, honours change, and preserves dignity.

This is not idealism, it is adaptation.

Because human life is changing, And relationships must change with it.

Final Reflection

This book has not been about love.

It has been about structure.

It has not been about finding someone.

It has been about understanding how

Togetherness actually works.

Human connection moves in seasons.

It begins in curiosity.

It seeks alignment.

It grows through cultivation.

It drifts when directions change.

It completes when honesty is honoured.

It renews when understanding remains.

'Every season is necessary.

None is permanent."

Pain does not come from change. It comes from resisting it.

Suffering does not come from endings, it comes from beginnings

That were never understood.

This book does not ask you

To stay longer,

Love harder,

Or sacrifice more.

It asks you to see clearly.

Because clarity is the highest form of care—

For yourself,

And for anyone you choose

To walk beside.

The future of relationships Will belong to those Who understand seasons, Respect evolution, And choose togetherness Without fear.

This is not an ending.

It is a return—

To awareness.

THE SHARED EVOLUTION RELATIONSHIP MODEL

INDIVIDUAL (A)

(Whole • Independent)

- Identity
- Direction
- Values
- Growth Path
- Capacity
- Autonomy

INDIVIDUAL (B)

(Whole • Independent)

- Identity
- Direction
- Values
- Growth Path
- Capacity
- Autonomy

↓

SHARED EVOLUTION SPACE

- Chosen, not assumed
- Directional alignment
- Renewable consent
- Freedom with boundaries
- Communication as feedback
- Intimacy as expression
- Growth without control

↓

ALIGNMENT WEAKENS / LIFE CHANGES

↓

DRIFT DETECTED

RE-ALIGN & ADAPT

- Shared evolution Continues

COMPLETE WITH DIGNITY

- No blame
- No damage
- Psychological safety
- Sexual integrity

EARTH'S REQUIREMENT FOR A NEW FORM OF HUMAN RELATIONSHIP

Earth does not demand permanence, it demands balance.

Every system that survives on this planet does so by adapting, not by holding on.

Rivers change course.

Forests renew through cycles.

Species evolve by responding to reality,

Not by clinging to the past.

Human relationships are not separate from this law.

They are living systems.

For a long time, relationships were built for survival.

They were based on need,

Fear,

Security,

And continuity at any cost.

That model helped humanity endure.

It cannot help humanity evolve.

Earth now asks for a different kind of bond.

Not one based on possession, but on participation.

Not on dependency, but on cooperation.

Not on endurance, but on alignment.

In nature, no system is forced to remain unchanged

When conditions shift.

Completion is not failure, it is intelligence.

Human connection must learn the same wisdom.

A relationship that supports life does not imprison growth, it walks beside it.

When direction is shared, togetherness flourishes.

When direction changes, honest separation preserves balance.

This is not cold.

It is ecological.

This is not emotional detachment.

It is evolutionary maturity.

Earth does not ask humans to love less, it asks them to relate more consciously.

To enter bonds whole.

To grow without control.

To drift without blame.

To complete without damage.

To begin again without repeating.

The future of relationships

Will belong to those

Who understand seasons,

Respect change, and choose togetherness only where life truly aligns, this is not a new morality.

It is a return to natural law.

And Earth has always been clear

About one thing:

What evolves,

Survives.

www.ingramcontent.com/pod-product-compliance
Ingram Content Group UK Ltd.
Pitfield, Milton Keynes, MK11 3LW, UK
UKHW021341190726
13845UKWH00027B/660